Hard Time Praying?

A Study Course Exploring
Difficulties with Prayer

Raymond Tomkinson

MINNEAPOLIS

HARD TIME PRAYING?
A Study Course Exploring Difficulties with Prayer

Copyright © 2009 Raymond Tomkinson
Original edition published in English under the title HARD TIME PRAYING by Kevin Mayhew Ltd, Buxhall, England.
This edition copyright © Fortress Press 2019

All rights reserved. Except for brief quotations in critical articles or reviews, no part of this book may be reproduced in any manner without prior written permission from the publisher. Email copyright@augsburgfortress.org or write to Permissions, Fortress Press, PO Box 1209, Minneapolis, MN 55440-1209.

Unless otherwise stated, prayers are by the author.

Scripture quotations are from the New Revised Standard Version Bible, copyright © 1989, by the Division of Christian Education of the National Council of the Churches of Christ in the USA, and are used by permission. All rights reserved.

Cover image: Photo by lolostock from iStock
Cover design: Emily Wyland

Print ISBN: 978-1-5064-5927-1

Contents

About the Author   5

Introduction   7

Session One	Praying with God in Mind	9
Session Two	Praying Through the Gauze	17
Session Three	Praying in Hard Times	25
Session Four	Praying to Distraction	33
Session Five	Praying God's Purpose	41
Session Six	Praying with Props	49

For the people of the Arle Valley Benefice,
Hampshire, with gratitude for the
opportunity to minister among them.

About the Author

Raymond Tomkinson is a priest in the Church of England. Before his retirement due to disability, he was a parish priest in a number of rural parishes and, latterly, director of a Christian retreat center. In the 1960s he spent some time as a member of the Community of the Glorious Ascension, an Anglican religious community, and trained as a State Registered Nurse with the Catholic Hospitaller Order of St. John of God. During the first half of his working life he was a nurse specializing in the care of elderly people and in hospice care.

He now lives in Rutland, England, with his wife, Rose. He is sought out for spiritual direction and to lead retreats and is a Visiting Spiritual Director to ordinands at Ripon College, Cuddesdon, near Oxford.

Introduction

The Earl of Chesterfield (1694–1773) wrote to his godson that religion was by no means a proper subject of conversation in mixed company. Successive generations have added sex and politics to that received wisdom. Nowadays it seems that none of these is a taboo subject for discussion! It would seem that the only subject of conversation that *is* taboo in Christian company is that of the difficulties people are having with prayer. Perhaps it is like marital relations: it is a private matter between lovers and, in any case, the last thing someone with difficulties wants to hear is that everything is wonderful in everyone else's relationships! Perhaps also, like politics, it is contentious. Each of us has different experiences of prayer and we might imagine there is no other way to pray than our own. I have known Christians fall out with each other because they haven't liked the way the other has prayed. Worse still have been the occasions when one Christian has judged that another Christian's way of praying is dangerous, demonic, or in some other way offensive to God. Prayer is the communication of a relationship between God and his people. Encouraging each other in that relationship and helping each other to develop our relationship with God is a joy and a privilege and should be approached lovingly and sensitively, with respect for the wonder that is the living, praying soul whom we call brother or sister.

I am not an expert on prayer but I am an expert on having difficulty in praying! I am sure I am not alone. I have found, however, that people are reluctant to share their difficulties and their ways of coping with them. This book offers some reflections for those who are having a hard time praying, and the resource material at the end of each session is written to help individuals and groups to consider the difficulties encountered and to find new ways to overcome them. The book may also be of use to Christians who have recently undertaken a faith nurture course and who find themselves with new questions about prayer.

Having reflected for some years on the problem of openness and honesty about difficulties with prayer, I was delighted to accept an invitation to take part in a year-long "Prayer Journey" being promoted by the parish of St. John the Baptist, Alresford, Hampshire. I was asked to lead the Lent session and was given the title "Praying in the hard times." I focused my addresses on the premise that it is not necessarily hard to pray in the hard times but that we all experience times when it is hard to pray, whether the times are hard or not. This book follows the same premise. It is my hope that, by taking a closer look at what may be going on when we are having a hard time praying, we may find ways of overcoming the difficulties we experience.

Preparation for the first session

Bring with you a picture, drawing, or other art work that depicts God (as God, Other, Supreme Being; as Father, Jesus Christ, or the Holy Spirit). Think about what you find helpful or unhelpful about it and be prepared to share your thoughts with others.

Session One

Praying with God in Mind

Are there times when you find it hard to pray? If the answer is "yes" or even "occasionally," this book might encourage you to share the experience with others, confident that everyone struggles with prayer at some time. How you struggle and what you can do about it will depend, to some degree, on how you answer the following questions:

What is prayer?
What is God like?

When answering the first question, we may find ourselves giving an example of a way of praying. If we say that prayer is calling on God in time of need, we are giving an example of prayer. If we say that prayer is telling God how sorry we are for having disobeyed him, we give an example of prayer. We may find we have no language to describe what prayer actually is, although we may resort to a metaphor or simile to describe it: "Prayer is like . . ." You may have found one that helps when you are asked the question "What is prayer?"

I would say that prayer is the dynamic of our relationship with God. It is like observing two people in love. We might say that we sense "energy"—"electricity"—between them. Prayer is that energy.

To use another analogy, prayer is like the communication between the brain and the rest of the body. The electrical impulses that form this communication are always there and there are times when we attend consciously to them. Like the times when we are conscious that we pray. At other times we are not conscious of these impulses but they are still there. In a similar way, we are not always conscious of the interaction between God and us and yet this too is prayer.

Communication between the brain and the rest of the body can become impaired and the body functions less well as a result. There can be serious or permanent damage, but more often something can be done to repair the communication. It is the same with our prayer relationship with God; most commonly we may have some impairment but it can be fixed. In the way that the brain can sometimes find another way to get a message through to a part of the body, God takes the initiative to repair our damaged relationship, but it may be that it is by changing how *we* behave that the two-way flow of communication is restored. Difficulties with prayer have many different causes and many different solutions. In this book we address some of them.

We may take some comfort from the thought that prayer is as much of a mystery as God is! Before we can take a closer look at the difficulties we are having with prayer, and possible solutions to them, we do well to ask the question "What is God like?"

When Moses encountered God in the burning bush (Exodus 3:1-6), he didn't know it was God who was speaking to him. Moses asked God his name. In the ancient world, to know someone's name was to have power over them. God refused to give Moses his name because he would not be owned or possessed. He simply said, "I am Jahweh," which translates to "I am who I am." By not giving Moses a name by which he could be addressed, God remained, essentially, unknowable.

On a number of occasions in St. John's Gospel, Jesus speaks of himself as "I am . . ."—for example, "I am the bread of life" (6:35), "I am the light of the world" (8:12), "I am the gate for the sheep" (10:7), "I am the good shepherd" (10:11). In this way, Jesus, the God-made-man, reveals something of God. The "I am who I am" is revealed in Jesus Christ as the "I am ... " Jesus altered the perception people had of what God is like. He taught us that God loves us (John 3:16), and his disciple, John, summarized this when he wrote, "God is love, and those who abide in love abide in God, and God abides in them" (1 John 4:16).

The revelation of God in Jesus does not make God knowable in the sense that we can "second guess" him or predict how he will behave toward us. God will always be so far above us that we cannot know him and yet, through his Spirit, so deep inside us that we cannot escape him.

What we imagine God to be like will be influenced by the revelation of God which Jesus has brought to the Church as a whole and to us individually. Our mental conjecture of that revelation will influence the way we pray. Hearing stories about God or seeing pictures of biblical events may have influenced the mental images we have of God. Some of those images may have been helpful in bringing us to a living faith, but others may have been instrumental in making it more of a struggle to believe or to sustain our relationship with God in prayer. For example, Jesus taught us to call God "Father" (Matthew 6:9). Some people find it difficult to relate to God as "Father" because they have had a negative experience of their own natural father. Others have been liberated by the discovery of God as "Father" as it has healed them of a bad experience of fathering.

We know from Scripture that humankind was made in the image and likeness of God (Genesis 1:27), but, to some extent, our own images of God are reflections of humankind. As long as we know that they are only poor attempts to know the unknowable, we will not go far wrong. It will help, too, if we allow our images of God to mature and to be ever influenced by the Holy Spirit. That way we will not become stuck with unhelpful and redundant images. You might like to ask yourself about the images you used to have of God and the images you have now. Did you ever, for example, "see" God the Father as an old man seated on a throne with a long, flowing beard? If so, was that helpful and is it still helpful? Do you ascribe any gender identity to God? What goes through your mind when you pray, "Our Father, who art in heaven"?

In the Book of Exodus (20:1-17), God gave Moses the Ten Commandments. God made it clear to us that he would have us worship no other gods. He forbade us from making carved images to worship (verse 4), images of anything in heaven or on earth. In the translation of the Bible we call the Authorized Version or the King James Bible, the words used are "graven images." A dictionary definition of the word "graven" describes it as the past participle of the word "grave" and that, in addition to meaning "engrave" or "carve," it could also mean "to fix indelibly (in one's memory)" (The Concise Oxford Dictionary).

Let us reflect on the idea that God forbids us to worship graven images as mental pictures of him that are fixed indelibly in our mind. We might then ask ourselves why God might forbid them. I believe it is possible to have a fixed mental picture of God that, in some ways, becomes the God we worship. In the Ten Commandments God tells us why we are not to worship graven images. He says it is because he is a jealous God. We may be challenged by the language used here. Jealousy has come to mean something quite different. Perhaps it helps to think of God's jealousy as his burning love for us and his desire that we love him in the same way and to the exclusion of all others. In other words, we are to give him his "worth-ship" (from which we derive the word "worship"). If the mental pictures we have of God foster our love for him and if that love for him overflows into worship, then our mental pictures will not lead us astray. A problem occurs only when we have fixated on a mental picture of God which so fascinates us that we do not "see" God at all or we are incapable of "seeing" him any other way. This is a form of idolatry and may harm our relationship with God.

It may be that we are stuck, through no fault of our own, with outdated and unhelpful images of God and that we only realize how unhelpful they are when we are trying to cope with life crises. Childhood images of God, long-forgotten, can re-emerge at such times. They can visit us like the ghost of Christmas Past in Dickens' *A Christmas Carol*, rattling chains of doubt and fear that we thought had been shed long ago. My own image of God, as a very small child, was somewhere between Father Christmas and the Sandman, a nasty character who throws grains of sand in the eyes of children who won't go to sleep! This was not a helpful image!

Some people are haunted by images that characterize God as a capricious and vindictive monster who is ever ready to condemn. Some are stuck with a Christmas Nativity "gentle Jesus, meek and mild" image that is not robust enough to engender faith in a God of strength with the power to help.

Even when someone has spent a lifetime believing in a God of love and mercy, negative and distressing images can haunt them when they are vulnerable. I knew a very devout elderly woman who had spent all her adult life promoting the good news of Jesus Christ, and who, in the final week of her life, experienced serious doubts about God's love for her. She doubted that God could love such a sinner as she perceived herself to be. Her image of God, at that time, had become skewed and frightening.

One of the difficulties that negative images of God can cause in prayer is that they can make God seem unapproachable. They make us quake like the characters in *The Wizard of Oz* as they approached the Wizard's castle. We should always approach God with a sense of awe and wonder, but also with a quiet confidence born out of the knowledge that God welcomes us as beloved sons and daughters.

Sometimes it is necessary to work at finding new and more helpful images to replace old and unhelpful (even harmful) ones and to let God inspire us. It is important to break the habit of having an indelible and fixed image of God, especially if that image has itself become something of a god. Images or senses of God need not take human form. They can be abstract or symbolic. Remember Jesus describing himself as a shepherd, as bread, as a gate! Remember the description of the Holy Spirit as "like a dove" (Matthew 3:16 et al.). Try having no visual image at all and cultivate a sense of God's presence through sounds. For me, it is the sound of the wood pigeon in the trees that reminds me of God's presence! Try cultivating a sense of God's presence through taste or smell—"O taste and see that the Lord is good" (Psalm 34:8). For me it is the smell of linen dried in the sun that evokes a sense of God's presence.

SESSION ONE

Focus for reflection

In the year that King Uzziah died, I saw the Lord sitting on a throne, high and lofty; and the hem of his robe filled the temple ...

Isaiah 6:1 (but see also the whole of chapter 6)

Questions for personal reflection or group discussion

1. When you close your eyes and think of God, what do you see?
2. When you open your eyes and think of God and look about you, what do you see?
3. Do you ever have unhelpful, challenging, or painful mental pictures of God? If so, how do you cope with them?
4. When you pray, how do you address God?

Group activity

Share pictures, drawings, or photographs that help you to focus on God when you pray. Spend a few minutes discussing what helps and what hinders your prayer focus.

Suggestions for prayer

Almighty God,
you have shown us through your Son Jesus
that you are a loving and a merciful God.
May we always approach you in awe and wonder,
mindful of your majesty and might,
but also trusting and confident
that we are your beloved children.
Amen.

Lord, I long for a sense of your presence.
Help me to call to mind the last occasion
when I felt you to be near,
and allow me to abide in it
until the consolation of your presence returns.
Amen.

Lord, my whole being senses your presence.
Stay awhile and bathe me in your love.
Let me stay and sit at your feet.
Amen.

Key words

God, "I am," prayer, relationship, unknowable, revealed, images.

Preparation for the next session

Set a small table lamp in the midst of the group—one with a shade which allows a glimpse of the light bulb when lit. The shade will be used in a later session as a place to paste prayer petitions.

Session Two

Praying Through the Gauze

Consider the nature of love and of our relationship with God. God is love and love is not something we appreciate through a single sense; it is a multi-sensory experience. The experience of love is something we see, touch, hear, and taste! A relationship with the God of Love is nourished by communication, and communication is affected by emotion and mood. If, however, our relationship is solely a sensory experience, it may be too fragile to survive our fickle emotions and moods.

If prayer is the expression of the dynamic of our multi-sensory love relationship with God, what happens when our senses fail us? What happens when our emotions and moods draw us away from the Beloved?

In such circumstances we need to hold onto our belief that there is something more robust about our relationship with God than sensory communication. It is rooted not only in the senses but deep in the heart of us; deep in our will, in a place untouched by emotions and mood. We need to remind ourselves that we are loved by God, unconditionally, and that his love for us is infinitely durable. In order that we may reciprocate his love, God has planted the gift of love deep inside us. It is the same love. This relationship of love is maintained at the level of our soul by Christ who dwells in us. He maintains the dynamic of our relationship with the Father and he does so in the power of the Holy Spirit. Nevertheless, our relationship with God can be harmed in at least three ways.

Firstly it can be harmed by sin. When we are having difficulty with prayer—when we have lost the mental picture we had of God or we can no longer hear his voice or sense his hand upon us—it might be helpful to examine our conscience to see if there is a problem in our relationship with God caused by unrepented sin. If we take time to repent of our sins, the difficulty may be resolved.

The second way that our relationship can be harmed is connected to the first. We may be stuck somewhere between penitence and the acceptance of forgiveness. So then, if we identify any of the "symptoms" described above and if we are not conscious of any unrepented sin, it might be worth exploring if we have truly accepted God's forgiveness. We may have difficulty in believing that God loves us so much that he will forgive even the most horrendous sin in the face of true repentance. Until we can overcome this difficulty, we may remain stuck. Conversely, it may be that we can readily accept God's forgiveness but we cannot forgive ourselves. A sin committed many years before and long since repented may continue to damage our relationship with God because of the inability to forgive ourselves. Prayer at such times might be proving difficult and yet this is just when a prayer for God's help in forgiving ourselves is most needed! This is when the work of prayer is harder, but it is work that has to be done.

The third way in which our relationship with God may be harmed is related to the previous two. It is the problem of being unable to forgive the sins of others, whether they are sins against us personally, or sins against humankind in general.

On my desk I have three filing trays labeled "In," "Out," and "Pending." Things in the "In" tray are things to be dealt with, and the things in the "Out" tray are waiting for me to get around to filing them away. Some of the things in the "Pending" tray are there because I don't know what to do with them. They are unresolved or incomplete. I suggest that God has something like a "Pending" tray and he allows us to put things in it that are unresolved, including the difficulties we are having with forgiving others. Such things may range from the grudge we are still bearing against our next-door neighbor for the damage he did to our lawn five years ago to the sin of genocide committed by a nation under the leadership of a dictator. Leaving such things in God's "Pending" tray sets us a little freer to get on with our life. Leaving them there is a statement that we *want* to forgive and an acknowledgment that we need God's help in forgiving. It may be years later when we notice that, by the grace of God, the things we left in the "Pending" tray have moved to the "Out" tray.

So, then, if we feel bereft of Love, and the light has gone out in our prayer life and we find the darkness confusing, we might do well to ask ourselves if we are in a right relationship with God. We have all "sinned and fall short of the glory of God" (Romans 3:23). We all do harm to our relationship with God to some extent, but because of Christ's healing presence in us, our relationship is continually being repaired by him. It is an act of the will—a discipline—that we try our best to cooperate with that healing process. If we can say, hand on heart, that we have done all we can to ensure that our relationship with God is intact, and still we feel spiritually numb and God seems absent to us, leaving us disconsolate, we may have to look elsewhere for the reason.

Christian teachers have described the "highs" and "lows" of our spiritual journey in different ways. Some describe it as "aridity" or "dryness" in prayer. St. Teresa of Avila, for example, wrote of her 23 years of dryness in prayer, which preceded her great work of reforming the Carmelite Order. St. John of the Cross, using the metaphor of light and dark, wrote of the "dark night of the soul" to describe a frightening and challenging experience of prayer. St. Ignatius of Loyola, in his *Spiritual Exercises*, wrote of times of consolation and desolation characterized by occasions when prayer comes more easily than others.

For our prayer life to be healthy, we need both consolation and desolation, both light and dark. It is everyone's experience, including that of Jesus. In an otherwise spiritually healthy person, dryness and darkness are more likely to be a sign of growth than a sign of difficulty. It is always worth checking out that an underlying physical or emotional health problem isn't making it difficult to pray. Such circumstances apart, dryness and darkness are as much a part of our Christian identity as the moments of great illumination when our vision is clear and when, like the disciples who witnessed the transfiguration of the Lord, we cry out in joy, "Lord, it is good for us to be here" (Matthew 17:4). In between the dark night and the light of transfiguration there are shades of light and dark which characterize the ambience of our prayer.

Staying with the metaphor of light and dark, it is important that we understand that shades of light and dark are normal and natural and that we trust that the light or dark we are experiencing at any particular time has a purpose. We need to have confidence in Christ, the "lighting manager" of our soul.

London's West End is full of theaters offering productions that attract many thousands of people every year. As well as the storyline and performances by talented artists, audiences are treated to ever more spectacular special effects. They gasp at each and every technological wonder contrived to fire the imagination and to transport them to other worlds. A generation ago an audience could be delighted by a very simple effect: the use of a "gauze"—a flat and transparent fabric curtain onto which a scene is painted. When lit from the front, the gauze appears solid and the scene presented is plausible, but when it is lit from the back, the gauze is transparent and another scene is revealed. It all depends on the lighting.

There is a "gauze" that hangs between God and us. While we are here on earth, it is always there but sometimes it seems more impenetrable than at other times. We are more conscious of the gauze and of its penetrability when we pray. As with the theatrical gauze, what we "see" depends upon where the light is coming from. Jesus Christ, the Light, illumines the mystery of the Father who is hidden from us behind the gauze. The Light of Christ is constant but it suits his purpose to light our way to the Father in different ways—different moods, if you will. Sometimes his light is a searing laser beam that penetrates the darkest parts of our being, showing us our faults and encouraging us to face up to them and to repent of our sins. Sometimes it is more like the glow of a candle that softens the edges and shows us in a better light. His purpose is to present us to the Father in the best possible light. When we are "front lit," the scene beyond the gauze may be obscured. It is still there but we cannot see it. We look at the scene painted on the gauze. It may have been inspired by a story in one of the Gospel accounts or by something we have heard or seen. Christ has a purpose in encouraging us to meditate upon it. He focuses the light upon it.

At other times there is no scene at all, only darkness. We sit looking at the darkness like an audience waiting for the stage to be lit for the next scene in a play, our attention held, our memory holding on to the scenes that have gone before. The Light of Christ has not gone away but his light is focused in a different way. If the darkness is prolonged or the scene on the gauze does not change, we may find it difficult to keep our focus. We hold on, trusting in the "lighting manager." Remember St. Paul whose encounter with the Risen Lord was followed by three days of darkness (Acts 9:9). Those three days were, arguably, as formative as any other time in his Christian journey. It may be an important part of God's plan that we adjust to the darkness and learn from it.

Then, just when we think that the light will never again be restored, a new scene is illuminated and then, when we least expect it, the light moves to beyond the gauze and we are treated to a glimpse of the glory of God.

When we find it hard to pray in the ever-changing light of our relationship with God, we hold on to the constants and the consistencies. God is always there; he is no less there because he is hidden behind the gauze. This side of heaven, the gauze is always there. Its penetrability depends on where the light is coming from. Jesus Christ is our Light. The Holy Spirit is constantly present. God knows what he is doing!

Focus for reflection

Lord, it is good for us to be here...

Matthew 17:4

Questions for personal reflection or group discussion

1. Are you in love with God?
2. How would you describe your relationship with God?
3. Are you conscious of any unrepented sin? Do you need help to bring it before God for his forgiveness?
4. What difficulties do you have with forgiving yourself or others?

Group activity

Reflect upon the way the light of your table lamp shines through the "gauze" of the shade. Christ is the Light of the World, but what kind of light describes him? Change the ambience of the room in which you are meeting to illustrate your conclusions about the Christ as Light.

Suggestions for prayer

Lord Jesus, you are the Light of the World
and you illumine our way to the Father.
By your love and compassion,
soften the light as you present us to the Father
so that our unworthiness may not be so obvious.
Amen.

Lord Jesus Christ, you have shown us the Father.
The more we learn about you,
the more we learn about him.
Open our hearts, by the Holy Spirit,
to make you ever welcome in our life here on earth,
even as you welcome us to share your life in heaven.
Amen.

Lord, I long for a time of consolation in prayer:
to sense your presence (*once more*);
to bathe in dappled light.
It would be a foretaste of the light of heaven
where no shadow falls
and there are no times of desolation.
Amen.

Come, Lord Jesus!
Amen.

Key words

Love, sin, forgiveness, acceptance, pending, consolation, desolation, dryness.

Preparation for the next session

Bring with you newspaper clippings of stories of people who are having a hard time. The host could provide large sheets of paper and glue so that a collage can be created.

Session Three
Praying in Hard Times

In an otherwise spiritually healthy person, a time of darkness, desolation, or dryness is more likely to be a sign of growth than a sign of failing faith. But what if there has been no consolation in prayer for a long time and the darkness, the desolation, and the dryness have disabled us? As a friend of mine put it, "Prayer is like screaming into a concrete bucket; you don't even get the echo back."

At such times it is worth considering our life circumstances. In a previous session we explored how a difficulty in our relationship with God may be adversely affecting our prayer, and how the relationship may be damaged by sin or by unhelpful mental images. In this session we look for evidence of other difficulties.

Prayer is not just the expression of a lifelong relationship with God; it stretches into eternity. We can allow ourselves to take the long-term view. We might adopt the same approach to prayer. A lifelong relationship with God, expressed by prayer, should change continually, reflecting the way our life changes. Prayer should mature as we mature. That is why, to some extent, the prayers of our childhood, repeated parrot-fashion in our mature years, may not express all we need to express, but they might be all we can manage just now. If we are trying our best to express more than that, and if we are trying to be honest with God, we need not worry. God knows our intention; the sentiments of our heart, crudely expressed or hardly expressed at all, speak loudly and clearly to him.

HARD TIME PRAYING?

How we come before God in prayer should reflect how we are. Perhaps that seems too obvious a statement to make, and yet there is a danger that we come before God being less than honest about how life is right now. We might use "tidy" or special language as if we were entertaining a classy visitor in the living room. We might play down our own feelings because we think that God will be offended by the way we would express those feelings to him. We may feel that our own life problems are trivial compared with those of others and that it is self-indulgent to bring them before God in prayer.

We should take comfort from the fact that we are even thinking about bringing ourselves and our troubles before God, no matter how inadequately we express them. The desire to bring them to God is his gift in us. He has never said that we should be eloquent, but he does want us to be honest with him. We just hold on to the wonder that we even give God a thought when we are so overwhelmed by troubles. What are these troubles? Perhaps we call them "hard times."

The cover of one edition of Charles Dickens' *Hard Times* describes the novel as a "withering portrait of a Lancashire mill town in the 1840s" in which the author "stigmatised the prevalent philosophy of utilitarianism which, whether in school or factory, allowed human beings to be caged in a dreary scenery of brick terraces and foul chimneys, to be enslaved to machines, and reduced to numbers." Does that sound like your hard times? Perhaps not, but you and I could share a catalogue of the hard times we have known or of the hard times experienced by people we know or the hard times we know about through the media. They are times of "trouble, sorrow, need, sickness, or any other adversity" (*Book of Common Prayer*). What adversities have we known in our own life or in the lives of others? Bereavement, divorce, unemployment, imprisonment, debt, poverty, failure, insomnia, slavery, abuse, exploitation, bullying, scorn, derision? Try not to sink into a gloom as you add to the list!

Is it really difficult to pray in such hard times? Christians turn out in great numbers to pray for a particular need. Church service registers show that congregations grow in times of war as people bring their loving concern before God, along with their prayers for peace and safety. People who do not regard themselves as religious admit to praying in times of great need. Prayer in hard times seems to present few difficulties. Perhaps the real question is *what* should I pray, or *how* should I pray in the hard times?

My first suggestion for praying in hard times is that we pray with others or, if we can, encourage people to pray on our behalf. When people are newly bereaved, for example, there is so much to do, so much to decide. There are arrangements to make. There are visitors to accommodate and endless refreshments to provide. People ask what they can do to help. They need to do something because they feel so helpless. They cannot do the one thing that is wanted most: to bring back the one who has been lost. There are things people *can* do to help. Some tasks are gladly delegated; other tasks need to be done by the bereaved themselves because those tasks help to ease the pain or provide a few moments of welcome distraction from the awfulness of the situation. Following the funeral the bereaved begin to find the energy to write letters to thank people for being there for them. They thank them for their prayers and only then do they realize just how scant their own prayers have been; how sorrow has been so deep that any kind of prayer has seemed to be beyond them or else it has seemed facile or trite or clichéd. As they recall the tokens of thoughts and prayers expressed in cards and flowers and sensible casseroles, they begin to realize just how "held" they have been. They begin to appreciate that the prayers of others have more than made up for their own inability to express themselves adequately in prayer.

St. Paul encourages the Church to pray without ceasing (1 Thessalonians 5:17). His teaching puts me in mind of a vast choir. The conductor asks one of the singers to sing a single note and to sustain it. She manages to hold the note for quite a few seconds, perhaps more than a minute, but falters when she needs to take a breath. The same conductor asks the whole choir to sing the same single note and they sustain it for hours because each singer draws breath when they need to do so and relies on other singers to sustain the note when they cannot. Surely St. Paul's injunction to pray without ceasing was given to the body of the faithful, not to individuals within it? Alone we may feel powerless, but together we can be a force to be reckoned with!

My second suggestion for praying in hard times is that we persist in prayer. The purpose of this is not that we badger God into answering our prayer. There is no need for that, but persistence in prayer in hard times is a way of staying close to God, of "logging in." It can also allow God the opportunity to change the way we think about the hard time we are having and to help us to find solutions or new energy to change the circumstances we are in. The only disadvantage of this is that we may feel, more acutely, the apparent lack of answer to our prayer.

Perhaps the story Jesus told of the widow who came before a judge for justice might help us to explore this topic further (Luke 18:1-8). This parable has long been held by the Church as a teaching by Jesus about persistence in prayer. The gist of the message is: persist in our request long enough and God will answer. The key verse is: "And will not God grant justice to his chosen ones who cry to him day and night? Will he delay long in helping them?" (verse 7).

It is a question, not a statement, but it is a reasoned question. If earthly judges are fickle and capricious and need persuading or bribing (as many did), surely God, the only wise and just judge, will not fail to hear the petition of those who are faithful to him. But what does this parable say about God? That because he loves us we have no need to make a nuisance of ourselves? Surely he does not need his arm twisted(?) to hear our cry for justice for the world or for ourselves?

The problem we are left with is that, although we might feel that we are on good terms with God, and although we do believe he hears our cry day and night, sometimes he seems to do nothing about it.

Once, when my wife, Rose, was a hospital ward sister, she cried out to her manager for justice for elderly patients in need of basic facilities. Her manager replied, "I hear what you're saying, Rose." Rose, in full voice by then, exclaimed, "Yes, you're hearing what I am saying, but are you going to do anything about it?" Perhaps that is what we want to say to God when the petitions of our heart seem to go unanswered.

We are taught that God always answers prayer. To say that he does sometimes and not at other times suggests that, like the judge in the parable, he is fickle and capricious, and that does not fit with our belief in a consistent God.

We are reluctant to conclude that no obvious answer to our prayer is no answer at all. The apparent absence of answer *is* an answer in itself, but it may not be one we want to hear. Does the prayer, "Lord, I have been really selfish, haven't I?" require an answer other than no answer at all?

On the other hand, we may conclude that because we don't like the answer we get, there has been no answer. It's like the old joke about the man clinging to the edge of a very high cliff. He cries, "Is there anyone to help me?" God replies, "I will help you. Trust me. Let go of the cliff and I will save you." The man thinks for a moment and cries, "Is there anyone else there to help me!"

When we don't appear to get an answer to prayer we might be tempted to give up praying and to seek the answer in tea leaves or crystal balls or horoscopes. But we may conclude, more healthily, that God *has* heard us but he wants us to persist in that prayer in order that he may test our conviction. We may conclude that he wants to be sure that our petition was not just a casual whim of a prayer tossed up into the heavenly places, half-heartedly, one wet Wednesday afternoon. Persistence in prayer shows endurance, tenacity, and character.

These strong virtues and attributes are part of the stock-in-trade for a Christian. They are part of the empowering of the Spirit that comes to us through Baptism and at other times when God feels we need a little more "oomph" in order to serve his purposes, and they are given to us as a body as well as individually.

God does not disclose all his purpose to us at once but reveals his plan in proportion to our ability to receive it and our commitment to fulfill it. He does need to know that we can be constant, in season and out; persistent in our determination to help bring about his kingdom on earth.

Persistence in prayer can show determination to become more like Christ, whose prayer for us is unceasing (Hebrews 7:25). Praying in hard times need not be difficult if we understand that even our unspoken anguish is a prayer to God. We need to remember that we are held by the prayers of others, and that persistence in prayer will change the way things are for us and for others. It is not necessarily hard to pray in the hard times but we will experience times when it is hard to pray, whether the times are hard or not.

Focus for reflection

Out of the depths I cry to you, O Lord. Lord, hear my voice!

Psalm 130: 1, 2a

Questions for personal reflection or group discussion

1. Think back to the hardest time of your life. Was it hard to pray or just hard to know *how* or *what* to pray?
2. Are you reluctant to bring your troubles to God because they seem trivial compared with those of others? If so, why do you think that way?
3. Do you find it difficult to ask others to pray for you? If so, why?
4. When God sends help, do you look around you for more attractive help?
5. Who could help you with difficulties with prayer?

Group activity

Share around and discuss in pairs the newspaper clippings you have brought along. Paste them into a collage of the figure of Jesus, using the dark and light parts of the print to make highlights and shadows.

Suggestions for prayer

Dear Lord,
Grrrrhhhhh!!!!
Amen.

Save me, O Lord, from sinking into a pit of despair.
Hear my cry.
Help me to recognize those whom you send to rescue me.
Don't let fear or pride prevent me
from accepting your help through them.
Amen.

Lord,
I am in such pain that I cannot call to mind fine words
or even express my need to you.
I don't know what I need.
Hear the voice of my pain—it tells its own story.
Ease my pain by your love and compassion
and give me some peace.
Amen.

Key words

Hard times, adversity, sorrow, unceasing, persistence, endurance, tenacity, determination.

Preparation for the next session

The next few times that you pray make a note of the things that distract you. Bring your notes to the next session. Is there something that symbolizes a distraction (like a portable radio)? If it is practicable, bring it along too.

Session Four

Praying to Distraction

Once we let go of the idea that prayer is something we *do* and realize that it is a relationship we are *in*, a time of prayer becomes a time of conscious encounter with God. If we stay for a moment longer with the comparison of our relationship with God to that of a human relationship, we would say that it is the Other who is courting us. The Other is God and he has shown us that he is prepared to come to us, not just to meet us halfway. God comes to us not only when we are strong and able to put in boundless energy to make the relationship work; he comes when we have nothing to offer, when we are weary and drained of resources.

Here we consider what we might do to enhance a time of prayer. To use a musical metaphor, once we know what song we are singing (and to whom we are singing it), we can focus on the phrasing of the music. A time of conscious prayer is a process. By that I mean that we enter a time of prayer in a particular mood or a sense of where we are before God. We should begin by noting what that mood or sense is. At the end of the prayer time we should note if anything has changed. When we spend time with God, the Beloved, we should expect to be affected by it; changed by it even by the slightest degree. For example, did we begin the time of prayer feeling angry with someone, having had an argument with them? Did we end the prayer with a sense of being chastened by God, forgiven by him; calmer now and with the grace to go and try to make up with the person with whom we had the argument?

If we are in a right relationship with God and if we are not overwhelmed by a life crisis, we may have a hard time praying for more mundane reasons. It would be a pity if precious time with God is being undermined or marred by a problem that could be avoided. We may be too cold or too hot to pray. It may be too early in the morning or too late at night. We may be able to cope with a time of prayer if only we can cope with distractions.

Let us assume that we are not in the middle of a plague of locusts but there is one annoying fly buzzing around in the space we have found for a time of prayer and reflection. What do we do? We have a number of choices.

1. We could include the fly in our prayers, give thanks for all God's creatures and turn the occasion into one of praise.
2. We could steel ourselves to ignore the annoying little beast and steadfastly complete our allotted prayer time, conscious of the activity of the fly but trying desperately to focus on God and praying through gritted teeth.
3. We can allow that the buzz of the fly is just one of many small noises in earshot: the gurgle of a radiator, the birds in the trees outside, or the spin-cycle of the washing machine downstairs.
4. We could remove the fly!

Based on the example of the fly, let us consider four ways of dealing with distraction.

The first way is laudable. Praise is a good antidote to all kinds of spiritual ills. One can never overdo the praise of God. Sometimes, however, we can use praise in order to block out the voice of God who is trying to draw our attention in a different direction. Praise away, but be aware of God trying to get a word in edgewise.

The second way is to steel ourselves to put up with the distraction. It may be just a device to try to turn an irritation into a virtue, like wearing a hair shirt. It may help a little but it may also prevent us from listening effectively to what God wants to say to us. Praying to God through gritted teeth is hardly ever helpful. It is not the same as bringing our anger and frustration honestly to God. That we should do! We need to draw a distinction between minor irritants that are distracting us in prayer and major rages that ought to be brought to God for resolution.

The third way is to allow distractions or incorporate them into our prayer. Consider the case of the employee who was sent to a training course because her boss hoped she would learn to manage her time more effectively. She complained to the trainer that she could not do her job because the telephone kept ringing or people would stop at her desk to ask directions. The trainer astounded her by reminding her that, as a receptionist in a large office building, answering the telephone and giving people directions *was* her job! Similarly, when we are trying to pray and thoughts of a particular person or circumstance keep distracting us, we should ask ourselves if that person or circumstance should be the focus of our prayer, rather than the thousand and one things we had thought were important to bring to God's attention at that time.

For those who are ill, anxious, or weary, prayer time may be characterized by chronic fatigue, pain, anxiety, worry, or fear. Such factors cannot be dismissed as mere distractions from true prayer. They *are* the prayer. Jesus said of his disciples, "If these were silent, the stones would shout out" (Luke 19:40). Read that as, "Even if I were to keep silent, my aching bones or my aching heart would cry out for me." To those who are wearied by pain, anxiety, fatigue, or whatever, many methods of prayer may be less than helpful. To them I commend what I call "the prayer of the lap of the Lord."

As you lie down to go to sleep, you may have brought to bed with you your worries, your pain, your despair, the guilt of things left undone or handled badly. As you lay your head on your pillow, imagine that you are kneeling at the foot of the Lord seated by you. Imagine your head resting on his lap. Smell the linen of your pillow and smell the Lord's garment. You have come to touch the hem of that garment, to find his strength, his healing, his forgiveness, and his peace. Bring to him all that weighs you down and feel the weight of your head on his lap. Don't fear that your weight is too much for him to bear. Remember he took the weight of the sins of the world upon him. Rest now and ask him for the gift of sleep. You have not stopped praying. Hopefully you will doze or sleep. You may not wake refreshed but you need not add to your troubles the anxiety that you have not prayed. Let the wonder of a twenty-four-hour relationship with God change your understanding of both prayer and of rest.*

In these circumstances we come to realize that prayer is no effort of ours at all. It is the Spirit of God at work in us, in wakefulness and vigilance, in rest and sleep: "Likewise the Spirit helps us in our weakness; for we do not know how to pray as we ought, but that very Spirit intercedes with sighs too deep for words. And God, who searches the heart, knows what is the mind of the Spirit, because the Spirit intercedes for the saints according to the will of God" (Romans 8:26, 27). Waking or sleeping, we become increasingly conscious of the God of Activity and the God of Repose. We develop another sense that utilizes all our senses. Perhaps we

---

* From Raymond Tomkinson, *Come to Me: A resource for weary Christians and those who care about them* (Kevin Mayhew, 2000)

call it numinous. What I mean by that is a sense of the awe and wonder of God, of his enveloping presence, of his power.

Sometimes life events or circumstances have a similar effect on us. Times of great stress or anxiety can be times when our senses are heightened. We can be hypersensitive to a clumsy word from a friend, easily moved to tears in the most unlikely situations or circumstances. Out of the darkness and the pain can come incredible emotional and spiritual growth. It may be some time after the event that we realize that the hand of God was upon us. We begin to see the possibility of the text from the Book of Revelation, "See, I am making all things new" (Revelation 21:5). This time of heightened sensual awareness is also a time when we can discover the presence of God. New senses are awakened, perspectives are changed, perceptions are altered. In this way we have not only allowed the distraction but we have (with the help of God) let it become our prayer.

We have reflected on many reasons why we might have a hard time praying and on what we might do to help ourselves. We have reflected on how God comes to our aid when we find it hard to know how to pray. We may believe we are on good terms with God, that there is no major trauma in our life and that we are not too tired or too sad or too ill, and yet distractions continue to make it difficult to pray.

We come to the point when we need to allow the distraction to be itself. Allowing it means acknowledging it is there, that it has a right to be there (like the sound of the birds or the rumble of the washing machine). These things are part of our life, and prayer should never be divorced from real life. We can learn to allow extraneous noise and to find a place of inner quiet where, in spite of it, we meet with the Beloved. It is the place of the "sound of sheer silence" (1 Kings 19:12). It is the eye of the storm. It takes effort and practice to be able to find it (even sometimes), but it is well worth seeking it. Finding it begins with letting go of the extraneous noises, not allowing them to impact greatly upon us. Some unwanted noises have a rhythm to them and we can, sometimes, adopt their rhythm and let them help us into prayer.

The fourth way of dealing with distractions is the removal of them. If you are hungry, go and eat! If you need to make a phone call, make it! If a noisy distraction can be eliminated it, eliminate it! This may be easy enough if the distraction is a fly in the room but other distractions are not so easy to remove. Into this category, however, I would put any strategies we use to minimize distraction such as choosing the place or time to pray.

We may say we have little or no opportunity for a time of prayer. People are worried and distracted by so many things, like Jesus' friend, Martha (Luke 10:41, 42), and to be like Martha's sister, Mary, and sit at the feet of Jesus feels like a luxury we cannot afford. In reality, we have to be both. Our human relationships exist whether we are directly in touch with one another or not. It is the same with God. In history, spiritual writers have always advocated that we cultivate a sense of the presence of God wherever we are and whatever we are doing and to be aware that we can pray anywhere and at any time. Like the story of the two nuns who each asked their spiritual director a question. The first asked if it was all right if she did the ironing while she was praying and was told that it was not. The second asked if she could pray while doing the ironing and was told that she could!

Focus for reflection

And God, who searches the heart, knows what is the mind of the Spirit, because the Spirit intercedes for the saints according to the will of God.

Romans 8:27

Questions for personal reflection or group discussion

1. What do you do about things that distract you from prayer?
2. Can you think of ways to minimize the distractions you experience?
3. What would help you to develop an "any time, any place" awareness of God?
4. Are you overwhelmed by weariness? What or who might help you?
5. Are you hypersensitive to images or sounds? Do they distract you from God or do they make you more conscious of him?

Group activity

Discuss the things that distract you from prayer and build a "Kim's game" table of items that symbolize those distractions, removing each item as you discuss it.

Suggestions for prayer

Lord, I do not know how to pray.
Pray in me to the Father
through the deep indwelling of your Spirit.
Amen.

Lord, restore in me the gift of awe and wonder,
that I may see the signs you send:
signs of hope and promise,

signs of love and mercy.
Use my senses to bring me truly alive to your creation
and to your presence.
Amen.

Lord of the night,
who comes to minister to me in my anguish,
let me sip the cup of your sustaining love;
let me drink deeply of your compassion.
Amen.

Lord, I am too weary to pray in words just now.
Let me commune with you in the night.
Hold me close to you
and let me sleep in you.
Amen.

Key words

Distraction, mood, praise, gritted teeth, allowing, weariness, sighs, Spirit, Presence.

Preparation for the next session

Bring prayer petitions written on sticky notes or on paper which can be glued onto the lampshade. Ensure that the paper is thin enough to allow some light through it.

Session Five

Praying God's Purpose

What is God for? You might think that is a strange question. Surely God is not *for* anything! God is God. And yet so often people pray as if God's sole purpose is to fulfill their requests. A friend told me this story and has kindly allowed me to include it here to illustrate a point.

A small child telephoned his grandmother to ask her to buy him an orange scooter for his birthday. His grandmother was not at home but she had left her answering machine switched on. The boy left her a message detailing his request. He was confident that he would soon be the proud owner of a brand new orange scooter.

The next time the boy visited his grandmother he looked around. He was clearly disappointed when he realized there was no scooter waiting for him. His grandmother explained that it was not yet his birthday so he would have to wait and see if he would get the scooter on the day. "Besides," she reasoned, "I haven't been out so how could I get you a scooter?" "Ah," said the boy, "but you were out when I called!"

Do we ever pray as if God was the grandmother in this story? Asking for what we need (or what we want) is not, at one level, hard at all. It is natural for us to turn to God in time of need, either for our own needs to be met or the needs of others. People with only the tiniest sense of there being a God cry out to that God in time of need. Volumes of prayer go up to God from all parts of the planet and the people of the earth make known their needs to him. Is it really that simple? Is it like ordering an orange scooter? I think not.

The small child did not get the scooter he asked for (at least not at that time) and we do not get all that we ask for when we pray. God, like the grandmother, knows what is good for his children; he knows that it is not good for us to get everything we want just when we want it. Jesus has taught us to bring our needs to the Father (Matthew 6:9) and he has taught us that the Father loves us and wants good things for his children (Matthew 7:11) but giving us good things is not, essentially, what God is for.

We need to go back once more to the Old Testament and to the Law of Moses (Exodus 20:1-5) to begin to understand that God is there to be loved and served, to be worshiped, honored, and adored. Jesus, in his summary of the law, endorses this teaching (Matthew 22:37, 38).

Our number-one priority is to worship God for his own sake and to want nothing in return except the privilege of doing his will. We come before a holy God and we become acutely aware of our unworthiness which leads us into penitence for the ways in which we might have let him down. Our hearts overflow with love and gratitude for all that he has done for us, and especially for what he has done for us in the death and rising of Jesus. Praise leads to contrition and thanksgiving. Only then do we bring our petitions before the Lord. It may be that we find prayer of supplication (petition or intercession) difficult because we do not let God show us what should be the focus of that prayer. We often end our prayers with the phrase "through Jesus Christ our Lord," but do we understand what we mean by that? One way of understanding it, especially if we are having difficulty with prayer, is that it affirms our intention to pray with Christ's own intention and then to ponder on what he is revealing to us at the time.

God sent his Son that we might know how to be more like him, and the more like Christ we become, the more we are lined up to the will of God. And the more we are lined up to the will of God, the more likely it is that what we ask for in prayer—what we cry out for day and night, what justice we seek for ourselves and for the world—is what *he* wants, what *he* cries out for, and what *he* seeks for us and for the world.

Through prayer he is transforming us (individually and as his body, the Church) and the more we are transformed, the more appropriately we will pray. Nevertheless, we may falter in our persistence in asking and may fail more often than not to line up our will with God's, and we may fail, more often than not, to understand that the apparent absence of an answer to our prayers is a lack of understanding, on our part, of his will and purpose for us and for those for whom we pray.

So often, one hears people praying for the needs of the world in a way that sounds like reading God the news, as if he doesn't know what is happening. For example, "Dear God, at 5:30 this morning, a gas tanker turned over on the interstate between exits 8 and 9. Please help the traffic to get moving soon. Lord, in your mercy . . ." Sometimes it seems that the intercessor not only wants to bring a problem to God's attention (as if he didn't know already) but in a way that also distances the intercessor from the resolution of the problem. Like the intercessor at a harvest festival service who prayed, "Dear Lord, thousands of people are dying of hunger and more will die if you don't do something about it! Amen."

The difficulty we might have with intercessory prayer is knowing what to pray, how to get it right. We have discovered there is no magic formula. We have enough experience of the power of prayer to know that it does change lives for the better, but not enough to make the outcome of prayer predictable. We know that God will not be second-guessed. How, then, are we to pray for the needs of the world?

In an earlier session I used the analogy of a theatrical gauze to illustrate a point about Jesus lighting our way to the Father. Let us develop the metaphor a little to explore how Jesus, who is our only mediator and advocate (1 John 2:1; Hebrews 7:25), prays in and through us to the Father for the needs of the world.

Let us suppose we find a place to pray—a place with minimal distractions. It is a meeting place with the God of love. We begin with adoration of our Lord God and we are conscious that we are on holy ground. We are in the auditorium of his presence and we marvel. Jesus has back-lit the Holy of Holies and we sense God's glorious presence. The light changes as we make an act of contrition and the light swells again as we accept his forgiveness and we give thanks for his goodness. Now the stage is front-lit and we see the scene on the gauze. The Holy Spirit inspires images of people in need, situations of tragedy, hostility, sorrow. We bring to the scene people who have asked our prayers. The scene changes continually and we hold our gaze on it for as long as it is illuminated. We can glimpse through the images, through the gauze, to our Father God and sense his response to what he and we see and feel. We need not heckle or shout or use endless words to explain what we both see. A deep sigh may be all we need to express what we feel and what we want for those whose needs are highlighted before us. God understands the prayer that is too deep for words. The light dims gently as we emerge from our time of prayer or it goes out abruptly when we are interrupted. We come away from this encounter with God knowing that we have prayed for others. We have not told God what to do about their problems. We have not judged them ourselves. We have held them in our gaze which has been illuminated by Jesus and have brought them into the heart of God the Father.

Afterward we may be changed by what we beheld. We may be spurred into action, with fresh inspiration for helping others. We may simply feel less helpless and more trusting of God.

When we pray with others, our time together could begin with prayer of praise and worship. We could move through prayers of contrition to prayers of thanksgiving, and then, together, we might "behold" the needs of others, naming them aloud or, if discretion is required, in the silence of our heart. Again, there is no need to "gang up" on God or to fight with each other to express our prayers more eloquently than others. There is no need to whip each other into a frenzy of clichéd epithets in the belief that we will gain God's attention more readily, or that we will solicit his aid more effectively. Remember that Jesus is in charge of lighting our way to the Father.

Focus for reflection

For where two or three are gathered in my name, I am there among them.

Matthew 18:20

Questions for personal reflection or group discussion

1. Do you tell God what he already knows?
2. When you bring a problem before God, do you also tell him what to do about it?
3. When you pray with others, do you feel inadequate in the face of their eloquence?
4. Do you join in with others to bully God into answering your prayer?

Group activity

Paste your petitions onto the lampshade and, in silence, read them. Decide in advance how long the silence will be kept. Someone could turn the shade around a little every few minutes. Afterward, share your experience of praying together in this way.

Suggestions for prayer

All praise to you, O God.
We worship and adore you.
You are worthy of all honor and glory.
The wonder of your love fills the earth as well as the
 heavenly places.
All praise to you, O God,
Father, Son, and Holy Spirit.
Amen.

Blessed be you, our Father God,
for you have rescued us through your Son Jesus
and have adopted us as your sons and daughters.
Help us to live a life worthy of our newfound
 relationship,
with the help of the Holy Spirit.
Amen.

Come to our aid, O Lord our God,
for we have sinned against you
and are not worthy to be called your children.
We are truly sorry
and we are resolved to lead a better life from now on.
Grant us your merciful forgiveness
for the sake of your Son
Jesus Christ our Lord.
Amen.

Thank you, Lord,
for all the blessings we enjoy at your hand.
We thank you for life itself with all its potential.
Help us to make the most of all you have given.
Help us to offer our life in your service.
For your name's sake.
Amen.

Key words

Adoration, repentance, thanksgiving, petition, transformation, mediator, advocate.

Preparation for the next session

Bring with you anything which helps you to pray. Ask friends from other Christian traditions to loan you items that help them (together with a brief explanation of their use). The items you might bring could include the Bible, crosses, crucifixes, pictures, icons, rosary beads, or prayer books. They might include items from nature or music.

Session Six

Praying with Props

The purpose of writing this course was to help people to reflect honestly on the difficulties they might have with prayer. There are times when we all get "stuck," when prayer does not come easily or when we cannot settle into a time of prayer. Prayer is privileged communication with God and it is his gift in us. This gift, as with all the gifts of the Holy Spirit, is to be nurtured. It is important for us to persevere in prayer because prayer is a staple part of the Christian diet, but there are times when our appetite for prayer is jaded. I have read many books on prayer but have yet to find one in which the writer acknowledges that we can become bored with prayer. Since I wrote that sentence, the ceiling has not fallen in and nothing else has happened to make me think that I have just incurred the wrath of God! Having considered a number of reasons why we might have difficulties with prayer, we arrive at the possibility that we simply have a hard time sustaining it.

I remember as a young novice monk that I was fidgety and restless during the early morning half-hour period of meditation. It was unusual for me to be fidgety because I was usually asleep! On this occasion, however, I was wide awake and aware of every spider on the ceiling of the chapel and every flick of every page of the pious books being read by the other monks, every cough and sneeze. I sighed audibly. I even tutted a couple of times. Eventually, the monk kneeling in front of me turned around and looked me straight in the eye. I said, "I cannot pray." He replied, "Just love him!"

Perhaps we will be kind to one another and call it "restlessness" rather than "boredom"! St. Augustine (354–430) suggested that our hearts are restless until they find their rest in God. We may need a little help in order to be still, and boredom may be contributing to the restlessness. This session is about finding ways to sustain prayer. Sometimes we need a few "props"—inspirational resources to perk up our spiritual appetite.

A wise spiritual director told me in the days of my youth that I should never think I am above needing a bit of help with prayer. It has been my privilege to meet many people who have a healthy relationship with God in prayer, and every one of them uses props sometimes to help sustain that relationship.

When I was putting my thoughts together for this session, I called to mind the many props I have used over more than half a century. Many of them are still accessible to me. I made a long list of them and of ways into prayer that I know other people find helpful. I was tempted to include the list here but I thought it might just seem like a mail-order catalog with an invitation to make a selection; I thought it might be self-limiting and prevent people from exploring all possibilities for themselves. Prayer is an adventure—like being in an adventure playground where there are many things to try. So, rather than giving a list, I thought it might be more helpful if I offered a few general directions to where one might search and find help with praying.

The first place to look is outside the confines of ordinary verbal language. I don't think we need too many words to sustain our prayer relationship with God. As a general rule, less is more! Language is so limited. How do we express, adequately, all we feel about God or the people and circumstances we behold before him?

Having stepped out of the general area of verbal prayer, there are two directions we might explore in our adventure playground. They are both rooted deeply in Christian tradition dating back to the first century. They might seem, to the modern-day Christian, to be associated with different and distant parts of the Lord's vineyard. They may seem contradictory. They are "silence" and "tongues." People may have difficulties with either or both.

There is a fear among some Christians that silent prayer is dangerous. A blank space is a gap into which a thousand demons may rush and corrupt the soul. At least, that is how it has been told to me. If I have misunderstood, please forgive me. Yet can the soul that yearns for God like the deer that longs for running water (Psalm 42:1) be so vulnerable in a moment or two of silence, a period of rest or during a few hours of sleep? It is true that many people find it difficult to cope with silence. Like other disciplines in prayer that we have considered, we might begin in a small way, with a few moments of silent reflection. It might be irksome at first but eventually we come to love silence and long for it.

The inability to be active in prayer opens the mind and the will to opportunities for contemplative prayer. It is a natural progression. One meets many Christians who have been vocal in prayer (especially in the early years of their Christian journey) but who now feel drawn more and more into silent prayer, meditation (prayer of the mind), and contemplation (prayer of the will). Fellow adventurers in prayer may be unaware of the privilege and the opportunities they have for contemplation and they may need encouragement and help to explore them. They may need reassurance that sitting still in silence before the Lord *is* doing something, and doing something vital for the health and holiness (same root word) of the Church universal. In the Church we have been very good at encouraging people to *do* things. We have been less helpful when it comes to encouraging people to *be*.

Language is limiting. How do we express our love for one another? If there isn't a word or phrase that adequately expresses all we feel, we are inclined to make one up. Our love language makes no sense to anyone else. It is the same with praying in tongues. The gift of tongues has meant different things to the Church at different times and in different circumstances (1 Corinthians, chapters 12-14). It is a gift of languages and is linked to prophecy for the edification of the Church, but it is also, for many people, a dimension of personal and corporate prayer. It is a way of expressing the inexpressible. It is a revelation of God's Spirit praying within us (1 Corinthians 2:10-16). It should not be feared. It is not a form of hysteria. Just because we do not understand it, we should not regard it as weird. In the 1960s and 1970s there was a new wave of spiritual renewal which swept across the entire Christian Church. Quite suddenly there were books on the shelves about the gift of tongues. In church communities where it had not been a feature, it was beginning to be openly used. People who pray in tongues are as diverse as the Christian faithful: young and old, Catholic and Protestant, extrovert and introvert. The renewal of the Church has brought tongues out of the closet but it is still the best kept secret in the Church. One meets people who say, quite simply, "Oh, you mean that bubbly little language that comes out of me when I pray?"

I remember receiving a telephone call from an elderly parishioner. She described to me how she had been washing dishes at the kitchen sink and had caught sight of a string of dewdrops hanging from the clothes line in the garden. With the sunlight glinting upon them they looked like crystal beads, and the sight of them had inspired her to praise God and she had found herself praying in words she did not understand. She wanted to know if she had just received the gift of tongues. Well, she had asked for the gift of tongues a few nights before!

One difficulty with the gift of tongues is that some Christians who have the gift can make those who have not feel like second-class citizens in the kingdom of heaven. No gift is higher than the gift of love and to make people feel that they are less favored by God is not how love behaves. We all have gifts but our gifting is unique, like our DNA. St. Paul encourages us to pray for the gifts of the Spirit (1 Corinthians 12:31; also 1 Corinthians, chapters 12-14). We should be grateful for the gifts God has given for the building up of his Church, and we should appreciate and celebrate all he has given.

In the gifts of silence and tongues, the Holy Spirit liberates us from the limitations of language. He prays in us at the level of our will, leaving us reassured that we *have* praised and honored God, that we *have* expressed our regret for sins committed. He prays in us in a way that leaves us with a sense of having thanked God for his goodness. The Spirit has carried us to the center of God's love with petitions on our heart and given (?) us a confidence that he *has* heard our prayer.

Let us consider next the value of prayers that have been prayed before. Some people are afraid of using pre-composed prayers, and yet great swaths of the Church use pre-composed liturgy to sustain the pulse of worship. To those who are "stuck" I would simply suggest the use of written material to inspire prayer or to express what we struggle to express. It is the disposition of the heart that matters most, not who wrote what and when. In this category comes Holy Scripture, of course. There is such a wealth of prayer in Scripture. Let the psalms express what we feel. Did not Jesus do just that from the cross (Matthew 27:46-48)? Remember, too, his own recommendation to his disciples in the Lord's Prayer (Matthew 6:9-13). We don't have to spend a fortune on what we might call "spiritual reading" but the purchase or loan of a well-chosen book may prove abundantly fruitful when we are having a hard time praying. It never ceases to amaze me how people of faith will spend money on all sorts of things but not on their spiritual development or nurture! We cannot buy faith but we can purchase an opportunity to be taught something new about being a Christian; whether it is a book or a few days at a conference or retreat center.

It was St. Augustine who opined, "To sing is to pray twice!" Hymns and songs can lift us into the presence of God. In times of dryness or difficulty we might recall the words of a favorite hymn more easily than any other form of vocal prayer.

Visual stimuli can be helpful in bringing fresh insights and feeding our imagination. Everything from a glorious sunset to the hand of a baby can inspire us to pray. For many people there is inspiration in the sight of a cross or crucifix, an icon, a picture, a statue, or other piece of art or architecture. Some are helped by the lighting of a candle.

Some people are wary of using a mantra as they fear the technique may have its roots in philosophies incompatible with Christianity. A mantra is the repetition of a phrase that expresses the disposition of our heart and aids concentration. The Jesus Prayer, for example, is a monologue prayer dating from the fourth century and originating in the Eastern tradition. In its standard form it runs, "Jesus Christ, Son of God, have mercy on me, a sinner." There can be nothing wrong with proclaiming Jesus as the Son of God and asking him for mercy. Short phrases of Scripture, when repeated reflectively, may be helpful in drawing us into stillness.

A mantra may be aided by the use of a chaplet of beads which keeps the hands occupied while the words on the lips set the heart and mind free to draw closer to God. The prayers that accompany the chaplet vary according to tradition (the rosary is one example).

The key to coping with staleness or boredom in prayer is to change something about our practice of prayer. Try a different translation of the Scriptures or a different version of a daily prayer formula. If you habitually use a prop for praying, try for a while using no props at all. There may be a need to abandon the props we have been relying on or hiding behind and to let God encounter us undefended!

The possibilities are endless. The adventure of prayer is full of unexpected challenges and delights. Regard it as an adventure both together and alone. Let us share our experience of the journey and help each other when we have a hard time praying. Finally, *enjoy* your prayer journey. Pray for each other. Pray for me!

Focus for reflection

O God, you are my God, I seek you, my soul thirsts for you; my flesh faints for you ...

Psalm 63:1 (see also Psalm 139)

Questions for personal reflection or group discussion

1. Is silence a feature of your prayer time? Do you want/need a little more silence?
2. Do you pray in tongues? Are you unsure if you do? Does anyone else know?

3. Have you invested, recently, any time or resources in developing your relationship with God?
4. Is your prayer life in a rut? What can you do about it?

Group activity

Discuss the props you have gathered, sharing your experience of using them. Encourage each member of the group to write down a resolution—a statement of intent regarding their practice of prayer. Discuss ways in which you might encourage and sustain one another in the development of prayer.

Suggestions for prayer

Dear Lord,
(sigh)
Amen.

Lord, still my tongue that I may hear your voice.
Speak, Lord, for your servant is listening.
You have the words of eternal life.
Amen.

Lord, set my tongue free
that I may praise your name according to your will.
I make this prayer in the name of Jesus Christ our Lord
who promised that what I ask in his name
he will grant me.
Amen.

Lord, I am restless
and long to find you in the still center of my being.
Help me to draw close to you.

Free me from distraction
that I may meet you in your Son Jesus Christ our Lord.
Amen.

O God, help us not to be too proud to turn to others
when we need help with prayer.
Teach us respect
for the ways you have drawn others to you
and help us to learn from them.
Your love for us all is infinite
and you have been wondrously generous in the gifts
　and resources
you have given to your Church.
Blessed be your name forever!
Amen.

Key words

Restlessness, boredom, silence, tongues, resources, mantra, adventure, alone, together.

Future sessions

Why not arrange to meet again in a few weeks or months to share your continuing experience of prayer? Hopefully, you will be able to share the joys of your adventure and will be confident to share, too, new ways of coping when you are having a hard time praying.

www.ingramcontent.com/pod-product-compliance
Lightning Source LLC
Chambersburg PA
CBHW071223070526
44584CB00019B/3130